~~I AM OFFENDED~~

DearUju

First Edition

Printed in the United States of America

ISBN: 979-8-9990740-1-0
Cover design by: The Author

"But I will restore you to health and heal your wounds,"

declares the Lord

Jeremiah 30:17 (NIV)

Dedication

This book is dedicated to everyone who has ever felt marginalized in any space. Please know that you are known, you are seen, you are loved, and you are enough.

I am deeply thankful for my husband, children, parents, sisters, and the rest of my family and friends. Your love and support, especially during the times I felt low, meant more than words can express. Whether through your prayers, kindness, presence, or encouraging words, you reminded me of the strength within and the grace that surrounds me. Thank you for being part of my journey.

Mommy, thank you for your prayers that helped pave a path for me to start my relationship with God. Daddy and Mommy, thank you for the sacrifices that led us to the life we live today.

I am also grateful for the temporary relationships that taught me how to love myself better.

May my God continually meet your needs in accordance with His will, and may He bless and keep you always.

Table of Contents

Note to Reader

Dear Reader,

Thank you for picking up this book. Whether you arrived here out of curiosity, a recommendation, or a deep longing for clarity and comfort, please know this space was created with you in mind.

This is not a book of easy answers or neatly packaged truths. It is a collection of reflections, wrestlings, and revelations born from seasons of pain, healing, and transformation. I do not write from a place of perfection, but from a place of process.

As you read, I invite you to take your time. Pause where you need to. Reflect. Journal. Pray. Cry. Revisit chapters as often as the Spirit leads, there is no need to rush. My prayer is that the words within these pages meet you exactly where you are and gently lead you forward.

May you feel seen. May you feel understood. And most of all, may you encounter the undeniable love of God drawing you closer to healing, wholeness, and complete freedom in Christ.

With love and gratitude,
 DearUju

"You have searched me, Lord, and you know me. You know when I sit and when I rise; you perceive my thoughts from afar."

Psalm 139:1–2 (NIV)

Preface

Mighty God, King of Kings, and Lord of Lords, I humbly stand before You, unsure of my purpose here, but trusting in Your infinite wisdom and guidance. I surrender this entire process into Your Mighty Hands, asking You to illuminate the path for this book to become a beacon of blessing in our world.

Lord, I pray that You guide its journey to reach its intended audience, touching hearts and minds with Your divine love and truth. May it serve as a catalyst for profound change and transformation, wherever it is needed most.

I ask that through the words on these pages, minds may be enlightened, perspectives may be renewed, and hearts opened to the movement of Your Holy Spirit. Let this book be a vessel of healing and restoration, drawing us closer to a deeper understanding of Your power, love, and grace. In the mighty name of Jesus, I lift up this endeavor, trusting in Your favor, provision, and perfect guidance. Amen.

My journey with this book began in 2023, but it was marked by uncertainty and hesitation. Although I had outlined its contents, I found myself immobilized, burdened by past hurts and lingering disappointments. I did not want bitterness to seep into these pages. But through prayer and reflection, and with the ever-present comfort of God's Holy Spirit, I began a transformative journey of self-discovery and healing.

It's remarkable to reflect and realize that I didn't feel like I truly began living until my 30s. It may have taken time, but I am deeply grateful that nothing I endured broke me. Thank You, Father.

Over the years, I have been surrounded by unwavering support, from my husband, my parents, my sisters, in-laws (and sister-friends who became family), and others divinely placed in my life. Their love, kindness, prayers, and presence were instrumental in my growth and renewal. For each of them, I am eternally grateful. My ongoing prayer is that I may grow in wisdom, stature, and in favor with God and with people all the days of my life. Amen.

To you, dear reader, I extend my sincerest hope that this book becomes a source of blessing and encouragement. May its words bring comfort to wounded hearts, clarity to confused minds, and refreshment to weary souls.

In *I Am Offended*, I hope to offer reflections that speak to the human experience, especially the pain of navigating spaces that sometimes feel unaccepting. I pray that this book creates space for understanding, healing, and reconciliation. May we be set free from harmful perspectives and mindsets that marginalize others. May we find the courage to look within first, to ask how we can contribute to healthier relationships before expecting others to change. And may we also discover the strength to offer forgiveness where it is needed, and to extend apologies where they are owed.

Let us make a daily choice to honor the humanity of others. Let us remember that every person's story is shaped by circumstances and a history we may not fully understand. Let us learn to love ourselves the way that God always intended, as we obey the two greatest commandments. And may we live out the teachings of Scripture, embodying the radical love of God, a love that transcends boundaries, heals divisions, and embraces all. A love that covers a multitude of sins, yet still calls us to truth, accountability, and transformation.

In closing, I invite you to embark on this journey with an open heart and a willing spirit. May the words within these pages bring forth a harvest of healing and renewal. In Jesus' name I pray, Amen.

Enjoy.

"Teacher, which is the greatest commandment in the Law?" Jesus replied: "'Love the Lord your God with all your heart and with all your soul and with all your mind.' This is the first and greatest commandment. And the second is like it: 'Love your neighbor as yourself.' All the Law and the Prophets hang on these two commandments." Matthew 22:36-40

"Bear with each other and forgive one another if any of you has a grievance against someone.

Forgive as the Lord forgave you.

And over all these virtues put on love, which binds them all together in perfect unity"

Colossians 3:13–14 (NIV)

Chapter 1: Call to Balance

"The thief comes only to steal and kill and destroy; I have come that they may have life, and have it to the full." - John 10:10

Jesus came to give us life, abundant and free, but many of us, though saved, are still living in bondage. We remain enslaved to unhealthy mindsets and perspectives that not only permit mistreatment of others, but perpetuate fractured family patterns and toxic traditions. These patterns, dressed as diligence or duty, creep into sacred spaces of our lives leading to weariness and wounds, not just in our lives, but in the lives of others around us.

"So if the Son sets you free, you will be free indeed" - John 8:36

I've been learning this: life in Christ is a delicate balance, a rhythm, leading to alignment with the Holy Spirit. It's not about perfection. It's about walking faithfully and intimately with God, learning to live in step with Him. It's about excellence that flows from our understanding of His Love, not from striving or performance.

Sadly, we often find ourselves reproducing the very wounds we've endured. Instead of interrupting cycles of dysfunction, we normalize them. And in the process, we unintentionally become the very people who wound and offend others, even in the name of service.

We may be quick to criticize others for becoming offended, but how often do we reflect on whether we have caused offense?

I'm not sure when the imbalance began in my own life. But in the early days of walking with Christ, I'd poured myself wholeheartedly into ministry while trying to show up for everyone else in my life. I was balancing a demanding job, caring for a toddler, navigating marriage... and I hadn't learned how to best serve those closest to me, the very ones I'm called to love and minister to first.

Because I didn't understand how to love myself as God intended, I became vulnerable to burnout and imbalance. This presented itself in my personal life as impatience, anxiety, and excessive stress. And in that misunderstanding, I allowed others, whether knowingly or unknowingly, to take advantage of that gap. I wasn't stewarded well by the people who should have been guiding me. And I wasn't stewarding myself well either.

Luke 10:41-42 took on a new meaning for me. In that moment where Jesus gently corrects Martha, telling her that Mary had chosen the "good part" by sitting at His feet, I saw my own reflection. I had been so busy working for God and His church that I'd forgotten to sit with Him.

Sometimes, obedience looks like slowing down. It looks like sacrificing productivity so I can sit beside my husband, watch a movie, and reconnect. It looks like spending time with my children, showing them that worship isn't just a song, but a lifestyle of presence, patience, and love. That is service too.

Even Paul was clear in 1 Timothy 5:8: *"Anyone who does not provide for their relatives, and especially for their own household, has denied the faith and is worse than an unbeliever."*

Our households matter deeply to God. Even scripture upholds the importance of considering the health of a leader's home life in qualifying them for church leadership in 1 Timothy 3.

I admit, for some time, I allowed myself to be pressured by others who may have meant well, but whose priorities were rooted in building ministry platforms and not fully understanding the responsibility of building people. In my immaturity, I led others from a place of striving rather than rest. I pray that those I may have misled during that time find God's truth and peace for themselves.

I've since come to understand that I need a sustainable, Spirit-led pace. One where I understand rest, serve my family well, work diligently, and still walk in God's purpose for me. These were lessons learned the hard way, but I don't live in regret. Instead, I hope these words caution and encourage you: it is not too late for the Lord to reorder your steps.

"Trust in the Lord with all your heart and lean not on your own understanding; in all your ways submit to Him, and He will make your paths straight" - *Proverbs 3: 5-6*

God loves you exactly where you are. I am deeply grateful that He separated me when I needed to be pulled away, and began renewing the mindsets that led to my imbalance. The Spirit of God is still teaching me how to live free - free from the religious burdens, cultural expectations, and anything that limits my experience of His grace and love.

Your walk with God should be most visible in your home and closest relationships. Not everyone around me is "saved," salvation is a deeply personal journey, but everyone should experience the same version of me, loving, consistent, kind, merciful and just. While settings may change, our character should remain rooted in Christ and reflect Him.

Remember, this is not about perfection, but progression.

There will always be needs around you. Let God lead you to serve where you have the grace and capacity to do so. But never forget, God's invitations are never laced with guilt, pressure, or condemnation. His Spirit leads us gently, not forcefully.

I invite you to call out to Him. Ask the Holy Spirit to guide you. That's exactly what He came to do.

"But when He, the Spirit of truth, comes, He will guide you into all the truth."

John 16:13

NOTES

"Write down the revelation and make it plain on tablets so that a herald may run with it."

— Habakkuk 2:2 (NIV)

Chapter 2: The One

Knowing God's love is the best thing that has ever happened to me. I love Jesus. He has exposed me, healed me, changed me, and transformed my entire world. He continues to show me who I am and walks with me as I become more like Him.

In His love, I've learned that I no longer need to strive to be loved, accepted, or acknowledged. His love is freely given and it is for me and you.

I may not have all the answers about the pain we endure, but even when we don't understand the "why," we can still trust the "Who." If we surrender our pain, sorrow, and hurt to Him, He can use it. He transforms our brokenness into blessing. He brings healing, change and reconciliation, not just for us, but through us.

God can teach us how to raise our children differently from our past experiences. To protect the innocent. To be present and loving toward those around us. To reject systems of oppression and marginalization. To extend acceptance to those who do not look, live, or believe like we do.

My heart sings:

"God I cannot believe how You have loved me, You have been so good to me. God, I can't believe how You love me. What a friend You have been."

- Been So Good by Elevation Worship.

This chapter deeply moves me because I believe it reflects the Father's heart.

God loves us all, all of us, more than we can comprehend.

"I pray that you, being rooted and established in love, may have power, together with all the Lord's holy

people, to grasp how wide and long and high and deep is the love of Christ, and to know this love that surpasses knowledge - that you may be filled to the measure of all the fullness of God." - Ephesians 3: 17 - 19

He cares about the things we care about. He doesn't shame us for having burdens or difficult emotions. He doesn't weigh others' hurts against ours to determine if we are worthy of experiencing them. Instead, He invites us to cast them all at His feet (1 Peter 5:7). We do not need to suppress our feelings or pretend we have it all together. We can bring it all to Him. He welcomes us into wholeness.

Are we not instructed to live by Jesus's example?

Our Lord Jesus shared His anguish with the Father (Matthew 26:38).

Vulnerability is not weakness, it is a path to intimacy with God.

In *Matthew 18:12-14* and *Luke 15:4-7*, Jesus shared the parable of the lost sheep. He described a shepherd who leaves the ninety-nine (99) to seek the one (1). This was not reckless, it was intentional. We have a Lover that faithfully pursues. God values every soul. He does not dismiss the marginalized. He seeks all.

Did we forget the story of the prodigal son in *Luke 15:11-32*?

The father didn't shame his wayward son. He embraced him, covered him, and celebrated his return. He also gently reminded the faithful son who stayed that *"All that I have is already yours."*

This is the heart of God for us.

But it also leads us to reflect:

- Are we creating safe spaces for the prodigals to return?

- Are we stewarding people and resources with care and intentionality?

- Are we equipping the right people for leadership? Or are we over-delegating and leaving the vulnerable behind?

- Are we attentive to the wounded who quietly slip away from our ministries?

- Why do so many churches allow people to leave silently... hurt, confused or rejected ... without seeking understanding or healing?

- Why have we normalized placing people in leadership who do not understand that pastoring is a sacrificial call, not a platform for prestige?

To shepherd God's people is not to elevate ourselves. It is to lay our lives down. It is about surrender. It's a commitment to nurturing, guiding, protecting and raising others up, with the understanding that the sheep belong to God. We are merely stewards.

It is not about power, control, or manipulation, but cultivation.

Not about authority, but responsibility and accountability.

Not about image, but compassion.

"Have confidence in your leaders and submit to their authority, because they keep watch over you as those who must give an account. Do this so that their work will be a joy, not a burden, for that would be of no benefit to you." - Hebrews 13:17

This verse is often used to call for obedience, but the weight of this passage is on accountability. Leaders must understand that every person in their care matters, not just those who are easy to love or align with their preferences. Leaders are accountable to God for the whole flock.

Are you a trustworthy leader?

Is love and compassion at the heartbeat of your leadership?

What does God require of us?

- To stand up for what is right.

- To be kind, even when it is inconvenient.

- To extend compassion, even when we don't understand someone's pain.

- To be fair, just and merciful.

- To walk humbly with Him.

- To stop chasing performance and human validation and instead embody the servant-hearted leadership of Christ.

We proclaim that Jesus is our model, but often, in our rush to do what *looks* right, we forget this vital truth:

Jesus always cared about the one.

"He has shown you, O mortal, what is good. And what does the Lord require of you? To act justly and to love mercy and to walk humbly with your God."

Micah 6:8

NOTES

(For your reflections, prayers or journaling)

Chapter 3: Beyond Denomination

I was born and raised in a Catholic family, and it was from this foundation that I first learned about God, reverence, and what it means to serve others. Whenever I visited my village, I'd wake to the sound of my grandmother praying diligently. Her voice would rise through the house at dawn, it was firm, unwavering and full of devotion. That legacy of faith left a deep imprint on me.

Several women in my family, my aunt and cousin, are Reverend Sisters. As a child, I looked up to them with wide-eyed admiration. They were the ultimate examples of selflessness and surrender, living lives that revolved around daily prayer, discipline, sacrifice and service. My mom's intense love of God, and the way she would cry out to Him when she was sad, left a lasting impression on me. As I write, I realize how blessed I am for being born into a line of strong women warriors. Thank You, Lord God. They have dedicated themselves wholly to You, and this planted a seed in me. I wanted to be like them. I remember vividly, going into the closet in my Aunt Theresa's house and pledging my life to God. Even then, I sensed I was being called to a life set apart. My Catholic upbringing ignited a real and burning desire to give my life to Him.

I praise You God for every prayer that my family prayed, for the ones I heard and the ones I didn't. I believe I am walking in the fruit of prayers spoken over our family line. I am grateful that I have the honor to carry on the same tradition, praying for and interceding for my own family and the generations that will come after me.

I have been surrounded by a faith rich in tradition, community, reverence, and devotion to God. As a young woman, I followed the full path of Catholic formation - baptism, Holy Communion, and confirmation - completing expected sacraments. Though I loved God and had a deep reverence for His presence, I didn't fully understand the person of Jesus or the movement of His Holy Spirit.

That changed in High School. I went on a weekend mission trip with my Catholic youth ministry, and during one worship night, with just the Youth leader Eric playing his guitar, the entire room was overcome. Tears streamed down our faces, hands lifted high and voices trembled as we praised God. That night marked me. I encountered the Holy Spirit, my soul recognized Him, even if my mind didn't yet understand Him. I knew deep down that God was Holy, that He was real, and that He wasn't far away, but near.

In the years that followed, I continued seeking Him... though my motivation was fear of missing the mark, God used that fear to keep me close. I remember attending a service in Seattle during a summer research program and being struck by the worship at the Catholic service on that college campus. It stirred a longing for more worship. Years later, that experience influenced the kind of church I would seek as an adult.

Over time, I visited many denominations, including Episcopal, Pentecostal, Anglican, and non-denominational. And what I have come to know is that God is not boxed in by a specific denomination.

- He sees our hearts.
- He responds to our hunger and desire to know Him.
- He honors those who earnestly seek Him.

"But if from there you seek the Lord your God, you will find him if you seek him with all your heart and with all your soul." - Deuteronomy 4: 29

In some Christian circles, I've heard the claim that Catholics aren't Christians. Yet, everything I know about Christ, what I've read in Scripture, what I understand, and everything I've experienced of His Spirit, tells me that claim is false.

Yes the Catholic Church, like every denomination, has its imperfections, but the presence of flawed leadership or institutional failures does not negate the faith of the individuals within it. Every church body, Catholic, Baptist, Pentecostal, Methodist, and others, has moments of missing the mark. God's grace has always transcended man-made walls.

This is why we must always remember: **we are the church** (1 Corinthians 12:27). Not the building. Not the hierarchy. Not the denomination. Us. We are His Body.

Jesus has never specified that He has a favorite religious denomination, instead He says, *"If you love Me, keep My commandments" (John 14:15)*. He says *"where two or three gather in My name, there I am with them" (Matthew 18:20).*

He invites us into relationship, not religion. Into transformation, not just tradition.

It is not about labels, buildings, or ministry size, it's about knowing Him, seeking Him and being so transformed by His Presence that others are stirred to desire Him too. You raise disciples more effectively when your life and actions reflect what you speak.

It's about glorifying Him and making Him known, not collecting followers for ourselves or claiming spiritual superiority.

Prayer:

Lord God, please deliver us from false religious spirits that twist Your truth. Free us from the need to divide that which You have united. Teach us to recognize

Your Spirit, whether it's moving in a cathedral, a tent, a chapel, or a living room. Heal our eyes to see Your Church the way You do: one body, many members, one faith, one Lord, one baptism (Ephesians 4: 4-6).

Let us be people who choose humility over hierarchy, relationship over reputation, love over legalism.

Father, please set us free from the religious boxes we have built around You. Expose where we have limited our understanding of You. Tear down the walls we have erected to keep each other out. Let Your truth rise above our beliefs and traditions. Help us yield to the transformation and healing we need so that we can truly operate as Your representatives on this earth. Let our worship be pure. Let our lives reflect Your mercy. Let our hearts be united in love. In Jesus' Name, Amen.

NOTES

(Use this space to journal your thoughts, prayers, or what the Holy Spirit reveals to you as you reflect on the chapter)

Chapter 4: Was Peter Racist?

Excuse me?

Yes, you heard that correctly.

Was Saint Peter, a foundational apostle of the early Church, a racist?

In today's world, conversations about race, discrimination and marginalization are unavoidable. They are everywhere, news cycles, social media, boardrooms, and yes even some pulpits. Some people believe that those who feel marginalized should move on from the conversation and stop playing the victim. Meanwhile, many who have been hurt are still reeling, disappointed that their offenders don't want to be held accountable for the choices that caused pain and devastation.

As uncomfortable as the topic may be, the Bible doesn't shy away from putting human flaws on display. It tells the truth about its heroes.

Let's look a little closer.

The Oxford dictionary defines a racist as "a person who shows prejudice, discrimination or antagonism against people on the basis of their membership in a particular racial or ethnic group, typically one that is a minority or marginalized."

Now, let's take that lens to *Galatians 2:11-14*.

In this scene, Paul recounts an incident in Antioch where Peter (also known as Cephas) was freely eating with Gentile believers, until some Jewish men arrived. And suddenly he separated himself from the Gentiles out of fear of criticism from the "circumcision group." His actions created division and hypocrisy, even influencing Barnabas. And Paul publicly rebuked him for it.

Peter's behavior?

- Prejudicial.
- Exclusionary.
- Rooted in fear of man, not reverence for God.

Based on today's definition, we could reasonably call his actions racist.

If you've ever felt excluded because of your race, ethnicity, or culture. If you have watched someone distance themselves from you to maintain the approval of their own community, then you have felt what those Gentile believers must have felt that day.

I have been there.

I have felt the sting of subtle separation.

The quiet withdrawal from spaces I once felt welcome.

The way people shift when their "usual" crowd is watching.

I have taken that pain to God, asking why believers, who profess His love and truth, can act in ways so contrary to both.

It is in that space of questioning that a truth was dropped in my spirit:

Being flawed does not disqualify someone from being used by God.

Wait, what?

Yes, it's hard to swallow. But this is where our human sense of justice must bow to His divine wisdom.

God does not operate like we do.

"For my thoughts are not your thoughts, neither are your ways my ways," declares the LORD. "For as the heavens are higher than the earth, so are my ways

higher than your ways, and my thoughts than your thoughts." - Isaiah 55: 8-9

"Has the Lord ever needed anyone's advice? Does he need instruction about what is good? Did someone teach him what is right or show him the path of justice?" - Isaiah 40: 14

God does not consult public opinion before using someone.

He looks at the heart.

He responds to availability and surrender.

"You will seek Me and find Me when you seek Me with all your heart" - Jeremiah 29:13

And just because God uses someone, just because miracles flow through their hands or messages through their mouths doesn't mean that person is morally superior or spiritually perfect. It doesn't mean that their every action pleases God.

Jesus said it plainly:

"Not everyone who says to Me, 'Lord, Lord,' will enter the kingdom of heaven, but only the one who does the will of My Father who is in heaven. Many will say to Me on that day, 'Lord, Lord, did we not prophesy in Your name and in Your name drive out demons and in Your name perform many miracles?' Then I will tell them plainly, 'I never knew you. Away from Me, you evildoers!'" - Matthew 7: 21-23

This verse stays with me.

It challenges me.

It keeps me honest with God.

I do not want to be a channel for His goodness only to be rejected at the end of it all. No way.

I pray: *Lord, let my life, not just my words, be pleasing and acceptable to You. May my actions always reflect Your truth and Your heart towards others. Forgive my missteps. Lead me in Your truth. In Jesus' Name, Amen.*

We live in a world full of noise, social pressures, culture wars, echo chambers, identity politics. But as believers, we must stay anchored to His Holy Spirit, Who is not moved by the spirit of the age.

We are called to speak the truth, but to do so in love.

To confront wrongdoing, but to do so without condemnation.

How difficult is that?

To love people genuinely, even when their flaws are visible.

Are we willing to be ostracized by our own communities to share the love of God with the marginalized?

Only the Holy Spirit can convict and transform hearts. But we must remain vessels who represent Him well.

So, was Saint Peter *a racist*?

In that moment, his actions were discriminatory and harmful.

And yet, God still used him mightily to help build the early church.

Even more, Peter repented. He grew. He changed. And God's grace remained.

This gives me hope.

We, as His church, are not perfect people.

We are redeemed, refined and renewed daily by His Grace, if we permit Him.

Prayer: *Mighty God, I pray that You will deliver us from every spirit that seeks to divide or diminish Your* *image in others. Break down the pride, fear, and ignorance that keeps us from loving one another truthfully. Help us live accountably and release the pride that causes us to minimize the impact of our actions and choices on others. Help us live boldly and courageously, overcoming the lingering past hurts and disappointments. Heal the broken or fractured places in us and make us whole as You intended. Let us reflect Your Kingdom, where every tribe, tongue and nation is welcome. May we walk in complete freedom. Thank You Lord for using us, not because we are perfect, but because we are willing. I love You. In Jesus' Name, Amen.*

NOTES

"Do not conform to the pattern of this world, but be transformed by the renewing of your mind. Then you will be able to test and approve what God's will is— His good, pleasing and perfect will."

Romans 12:2

Chapter 5: Lord, Search Me

"Search me, God, and know my heart; test me and know my anxious thoughts. See if there is any offensive way in me, and lead me in the way everlasting." - Psalm 139:23–24 (NIV)

This journey has never been about condemnation, but about clarity. It is about letting God search our hearts, renew our minds, and call us higher... into love, wholeness, and truth.

Offense loses its power when we let God perform the heart surgery only He is qualified to do.

"Jesus came and told his disciples, "I have been given all authority in heaven and on earth. Therefore, go and make disciples of all the nations, baptizing them in the name of the Father and the Son and the Holy Spirit." - Matthew 28: 18-19

Are we possibly losing sight of what Jesus truly meant?

Are we stewarding this mandate with humility and integrity?

"For Christ himself has brought peace to us. He united Jews and Gentiles into one people when, in his own body on the cross, he broke down the wall of hostility that separated us. He did this by ending the system of law with its commandments and regulations. He made peace between Jews and Gentiles by creating in himself one new people from the two groups." - Ephesians 2: 14-15

When we look around our communities and churches, does everyone look and sound just like us?

Is that truly what Christlike living really looks like?

Shouldn't we reflect the diversity in God's original design?

Shouldn't we honor the differences? Because why else would God have added these special touches to us if they didn't matter?

Take a moment to ask:

- Who have I excluded?

- Where have I aligned with comfort instead of calling?

- What is the Holy Spirit highlighting for me to surrender or act on today?

"Let us think of ways to motivate one another to acts of love and good works. And let us not neglect our meeting together, as some people do, but encourage one another, especially now that the day of his return is drawing near. Dear friends, if we deliberately continue sinning after we have received knowledge of

the truth, there is no longer any sacrifice that will cover these sins." - Hebrews 10: 24-26

Prayer:

Mighty God, demonstrate in and through us how You intend for life to be lived in Your Kingdom. Let us see ourselves the way You see us. Help us to honor the diversity in Your creation.

Teach us, Holy Spirit, how to walk in Your fruits - in love, goodness, kindness, peace, joy, patience, gentleness, faithfulness and self-control.

Strengthen us to persevere and to love as You defined in 1 Corinthians 13:4-7, at all times, not only when it is convenient. May we not grow tired of doing good (Galatians 6: 9-10).

Lord, help us to understand that the redeemed are not meant to be exclusionary.

Let us not fill our tables and gatherings only with those that look and sound like us.

Let us not lose Your heart for the lost.

Let us not create false doctrines that contradict Your heart. You always care about the one.

Thank You, Lord, that You are a just God.

Thank You for teaching us that You are the One who gives justice.

Holy Lord, release us from seeking vengeance.

Help us to forgive those that have wronged us.

Father, release us from unforgiveness.

And help those we have wronged to forgive us.

Thank You, Father, that You work all things together for good, so that we can continue to live out the call You have placed on our lives.

"And we know that God causes everything to work together for the good of those who love God and are called according to His purpose for them. For God knew His people in advance, and He chose them to become like his Son, so that His Son would be the firstborn among many brothers and sisters. And having chosen them, He called them to come to Him. And having called them, He gave them right standing with Himself. And having given them right standing, He gave them His glory." - Romans 8: 28-30

Thank You, Lord, that nothing is wasted in Your hands.

Father, help us to walk in true freedom and wholeness.

May every trauma and mistake of the past lose its hold and cease to have authority over our lives.

Thank You for the journey of freedom with You.

Thank You, Lord, that the same Spirit Who raised Jesus from the dead lives in us. And because of that, we know that the dark valleys can never be our resting place.

Thank You, Lord, for Resurrection Power.

In Jesus' Name I pray, decree and declare, Amen.

You are called, loved, and chosen.

May you continue to walk in the authority and compassion of Christ, remembering:

The Kingdom of God is not built on

preferences,

but on love. ❤

NOTES

"Create in me a pure heart, O God, and renew a steadfast spirit within me."

Psalm 51:10

"Examine yourselves to see whether you are in the faith; test yourselves.

Do you not realize that Christ Jesus is in you— unless, of course, you fail the test?"

2 Corinthians 13:5

REFLECTIONS

"Let us examine our ways and test them, and let us return to the Lord."

Lamentations 3:40 (NIV)

While prompts have been provided, you are encouraged to reflect freely, as the Spirit leads.

Today, I am asking the Lord to reveal...

Write three words that describe God's love for all people.

Do I reflect these in my own life?

Are there walls in my heart?

That block my understanding or experience of God's love?

For Him?

For myself?

For others?

Is there a name or situation where forgiveness is needed?

Write it down.

Invite God's healing into this space.

Draw your Kingdom table.

Who is seated at it?

Who is missing?

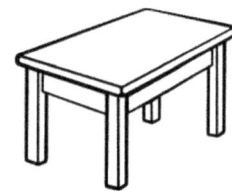

Ask the Holy Spirit to reveal anyone you may have left out - intentionally or unintentionally.

Holy Spirit, what are You saying to me right now?

Pause. Listen. Journal freely.

Closing Prayer.

What is your closing prayer?

(You may write it here or speak it to Him)

References & Pre-Acknowledgements

- **BibleGateway.com** – my go-to digital concordance and Scripture companion throughout this journey.
- **Google Search Engine** – for helping me dig deeper into biblical references and providing further clarity when I needed it.

- **Google AI** – for assistance with connecting the dots and helping expand my understanding along the way.

- **"Been So Good" – Elevation Worship (2023)** – a worship anthem that stirred my soul during this writing journey.

- **ChatGPT** – thank you for being my editor, sounding board, and clarity coach. You provided structure to the stirring.

- **The Holy Spirit** ❤ – the True Author behind every chapter, line, and revelation in this book. Thank You, Lord. All the glory belongs to You.

Final Acknowledgments

To my family and friends, thank you for your love and consideration throughout the years. Your kindness, graciousness, and generosity have meant the world to me. I'm so grateful for how our relationships have grown through different seasons. I love you all deeply.

To Nunu, thank you for every prayer and the meaningful conversations we shared about the heart of this book at its conception. I will always treasure you. Nunu and Afy, I'm sorry for the mistakes I've made along the way. This journey of life, of learning to break free, has been both challenging and beautiful. And I'm still growing.

To my amazing husband, Oge, Obi'm, thank you for your wisdom, your honesty, and your support through every stage of this healing process. Thank you for doing the hard work of walking through dark valleys into His loving embrace. Thank you for being a sounding board for so many of these ideas. Thank you for loving me, and for choosing to grow with me in God's love.

To my beautiful babies, thank you for making me your mama.

Ama, thank you for anchoring me to this world when I almost lost my way. Thank you for teaching me about myself and for giving me so much grace. May you always find His grace and favor wherever you go. Naet, thank you for being such a loving soul. You make me feel seen. You are an answered prayer. May you always worship God. May you both know Him intimately and walk with Him faithfully all your lives. Amen.

To the offenders I have encountered, thank you. Thank you for the hard lessons that have helped me grow in grace, compassion, and understanding. You've taught me how to love myself more fully, so that I can love others better. I pray that you find the correction and healing you need, and that the pain you've carried, or caused, will not continue to flow into the lives of others.

To those I have offended, I sincerely apologize. I pray you find it in your heart to forgive me. I also pray you receive the healing your heart needs. May we all live truly free in Christ.

And finally, the greatest thanks and praise go to my Creator, my Father, my Lover, and my Friend.

Thank You for Your constant presence.
For Your faithfulness in my life.
For giving me the courage to write this book, even when I was afraid.
Thank You, Jesus, for setting me free and teaching me

to walk in complete freedom.

Thank You for being the Great Physician, healing my

heart, mind, body, and soul. You alone can satisfy ♥

About the Author

DearUju was born and raised in Nigeria and moved to the United States as a teenager. From a young age, she has had a deep desire to help others, which initially inspired her to pursue a career in medicine. Though that path eventually shifted, she went on to earn a Ph.D. in Cell Biology, with research focused on the impact of specific gene aberrations on hematologic diseases.

She is married and a grateful mother of two beautiful children. Uju has a heart for worship and is passionate about honoring God in her daily life.

Her deepest desire is for you to encounter the fullness of God, in your heart, your healing, and your freedom, just as He always intended.

Instagram: @DearUju

Blog: DearUju.com